Jayden's Big Day

By Maurice Davis

Copyright © 2020 by Maurice Davis

All rights reserved. No part of this book may be reproduced or used in any manner without written permission of the copyright owners except for the use of quotations in a book review or for educational purposes.

Today started like any other day for Jayden. Dad is making blueberry pancakes and Mom is in the garden.

"After breakfast, can I watch something on your phone?"
"Yes, Jayden." Replied Dad

Just then, during the middle of Jayden's favorite show, a toy pops up on the screen. Jayden has never seen anything so cool.

Jayden screams, "Dad, come quick. I have to show you something."

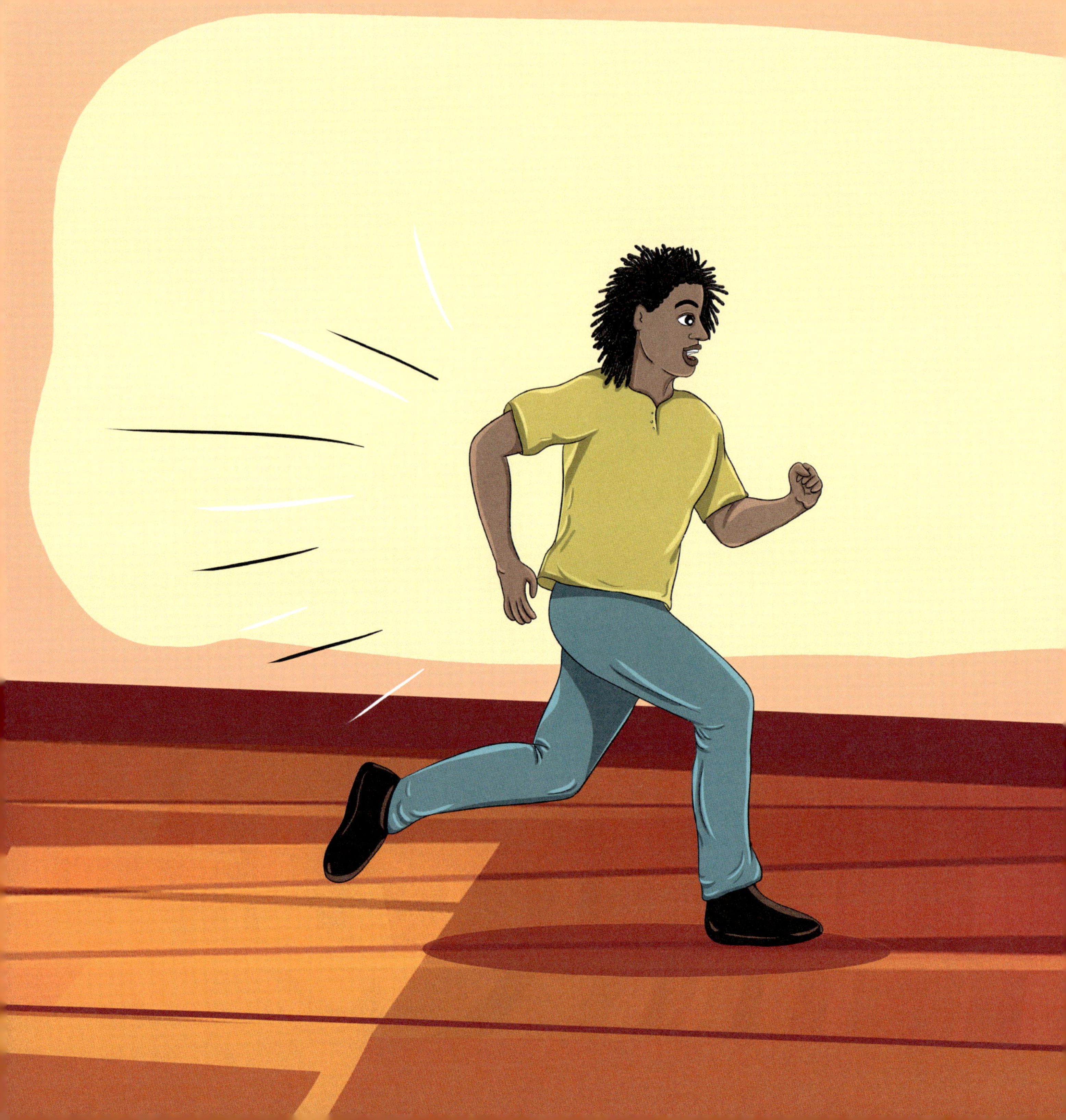

"This toy is so cool, will you buy it for me?" Pleeeease" said, Jayden.
"Jayden, I would love to get you that toy, but your mom and I don't have the money," Dad replied.

Jayden starts to walk away. He heads towards the kitchen, looking sad...

Before Jayden walked away, his dad said, "Jayden, once we have the money, I will take you to the store to buy the toy. I promise."

Jayden walks through the door with a sad look on his face.

"I know you are sad. Take this snack and go play with your friends. You will feel better in no time," said mom.

"how can I get money for my toy?"

"Hey guys!" Yelled, Jayden

Jamel sees the bowl of watermelon.
Jamal says to Jayden, "why do you have so much watermelon? Can I have some?"

"Sorry Jamal, I don't think I can share any today because we don't have any money and I don't want my Dad to get mad."

"Well, I have money. If I give you 25 cents, can I have some?"

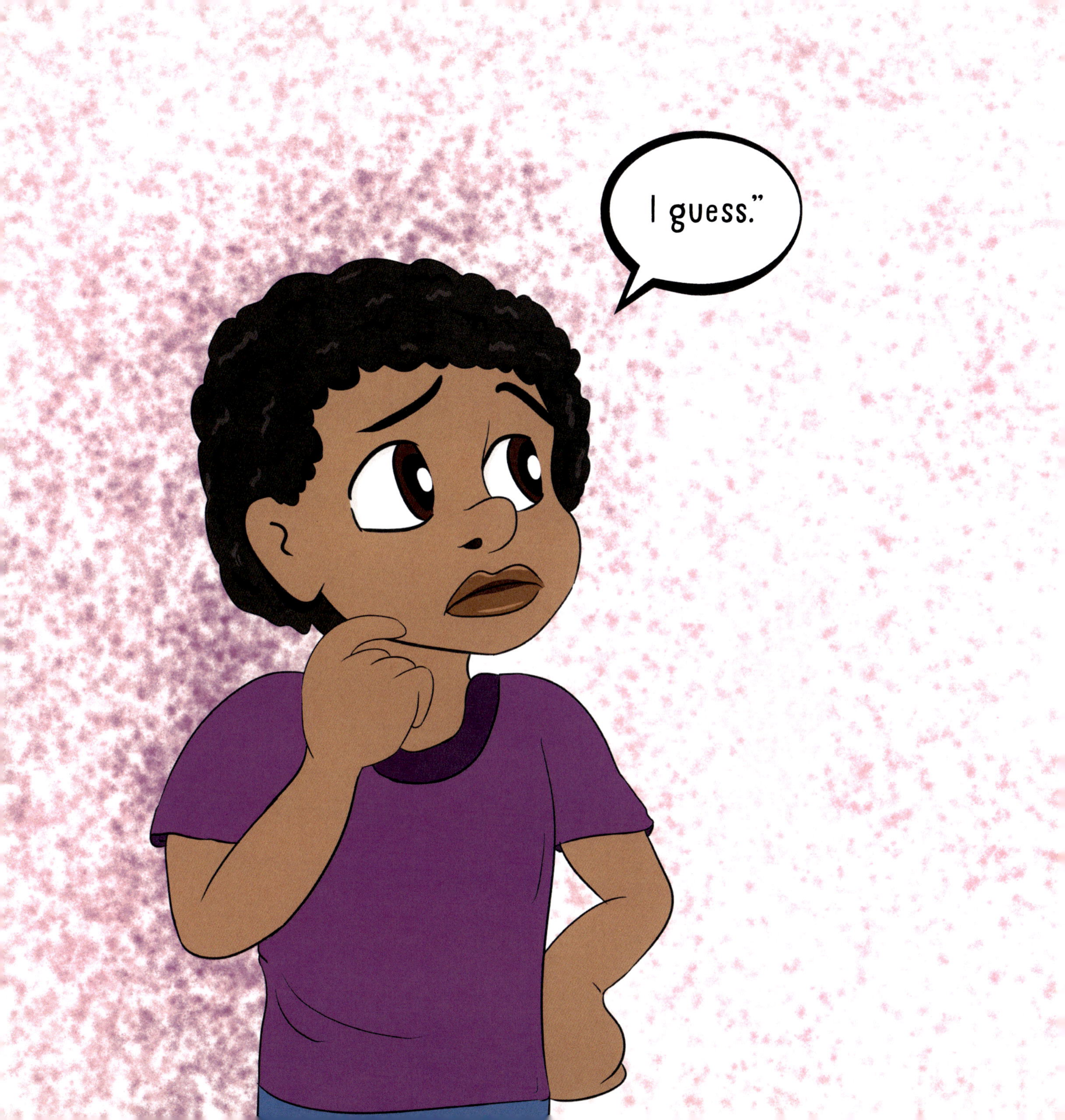
I guess."

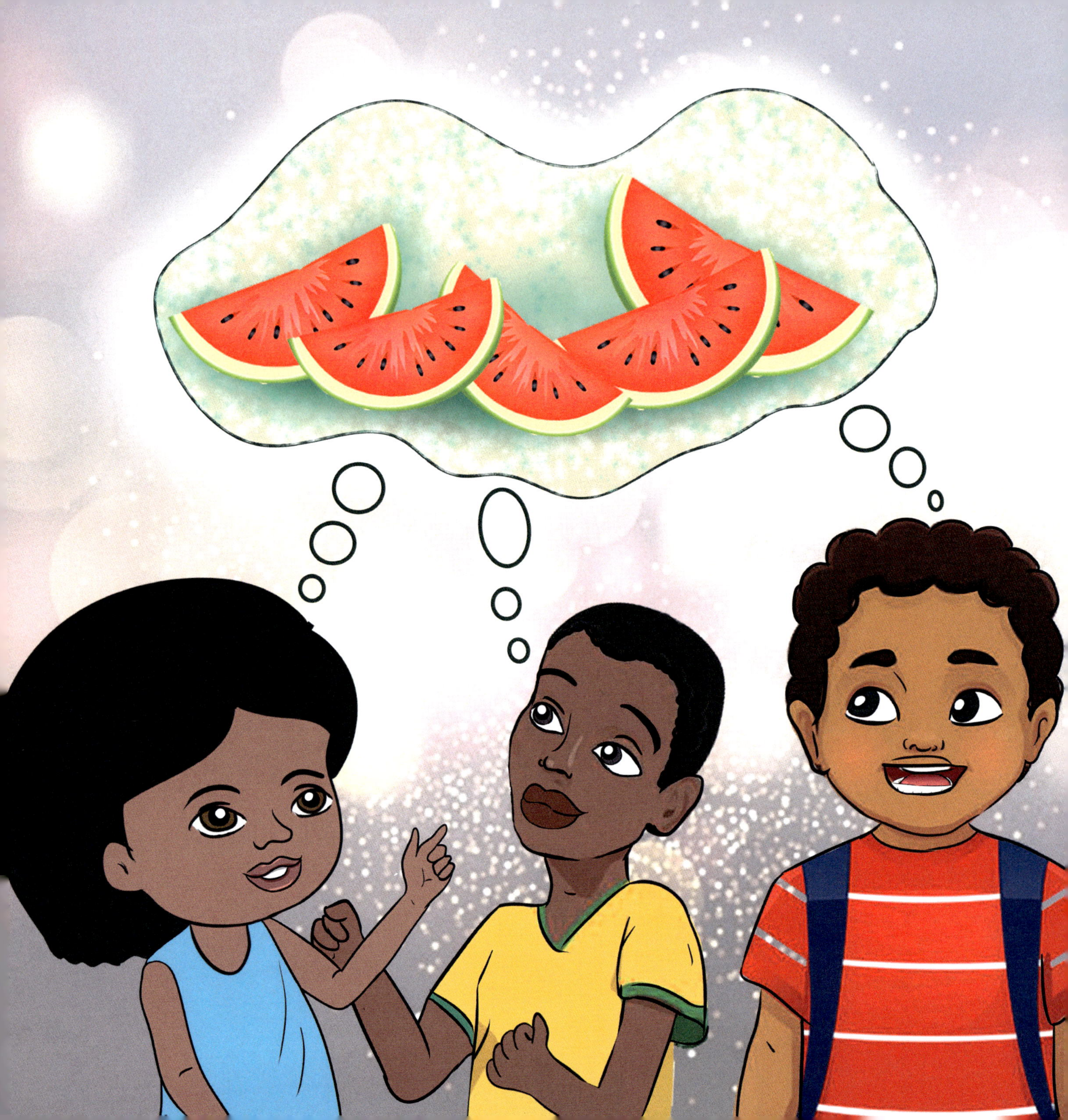

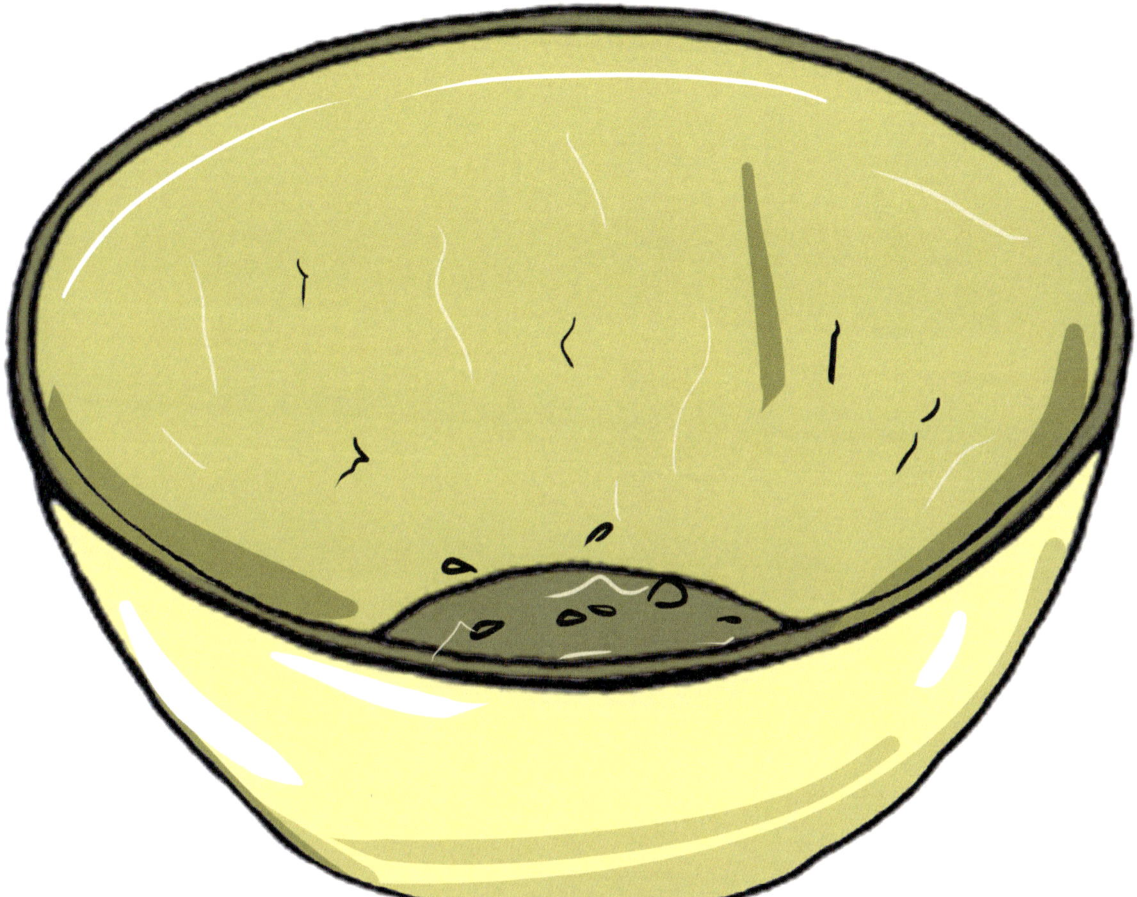

All of a sudden, it hit Jayden like a bolt of lightning. Thinking to himself, "If I get more watermelon, I will have money to buy my toy."

"Mom, may I have another bowl of watermelon?"

"Sure, Jayden. You can have as much as you want." Replied his mom. "You must be hungry."

With quarters in hand, Jayden's friends are waiting for him to return with more watermelons.

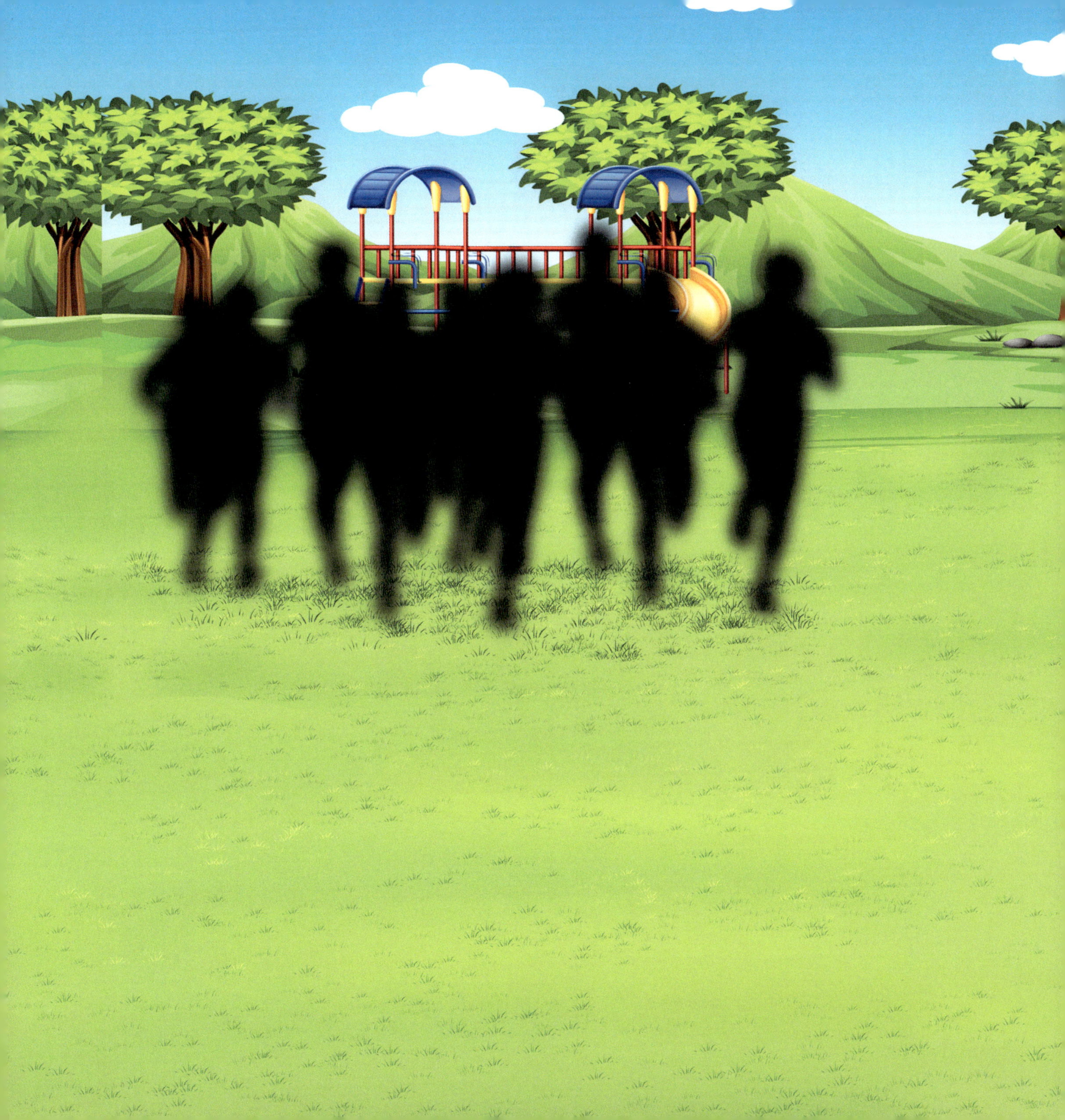

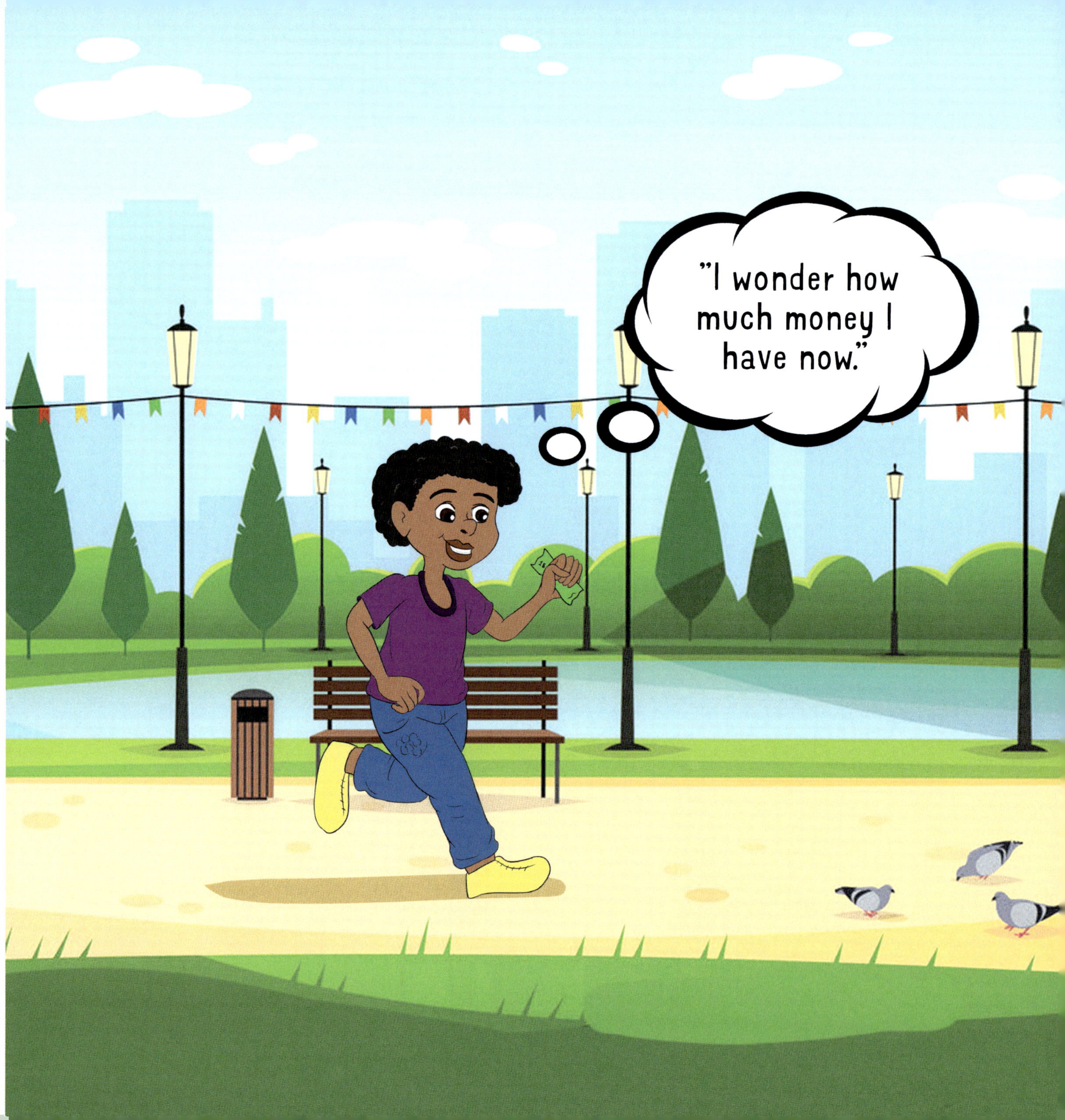
"I wonder how much money I have now."

"Dad, I have to show you something."
"Jayden, I thought we talked about this..."

"Jayden, where did you get this money?" Said Dad.

"My friends traded me for some of mom's watermelon," Jayden said happily.

"Do I have enough now for my toy?" Asked Jayden.

"Jayden, you have just enough. I am so proud of you." said dad.

"Well Jayden, let's go." Said dad
"Where are we going?" replied Jayden
"To get your toy Jayden."

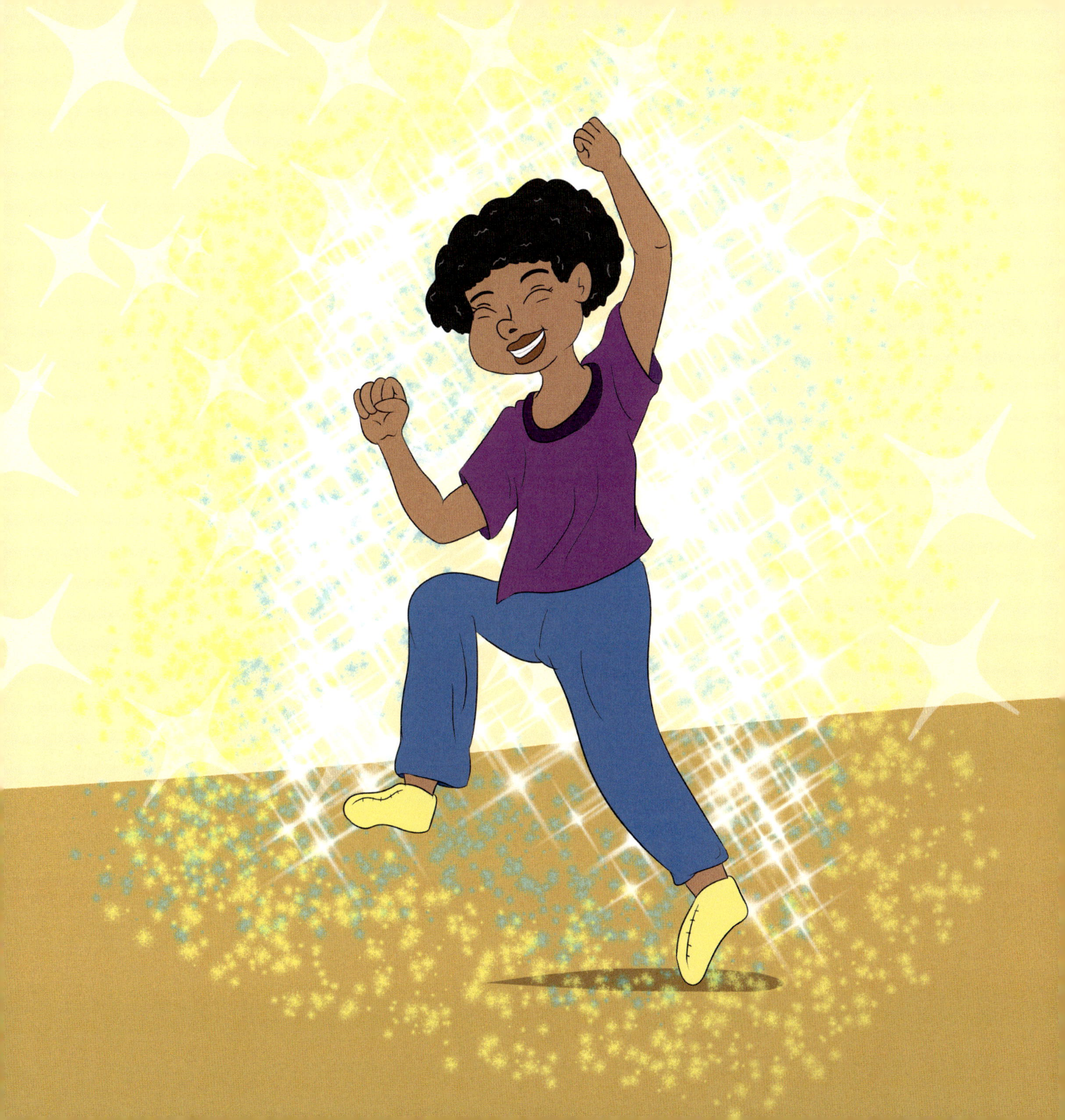

"it sure was really cool making all that money."

"Dad, there it is!" Yelled Jayden.

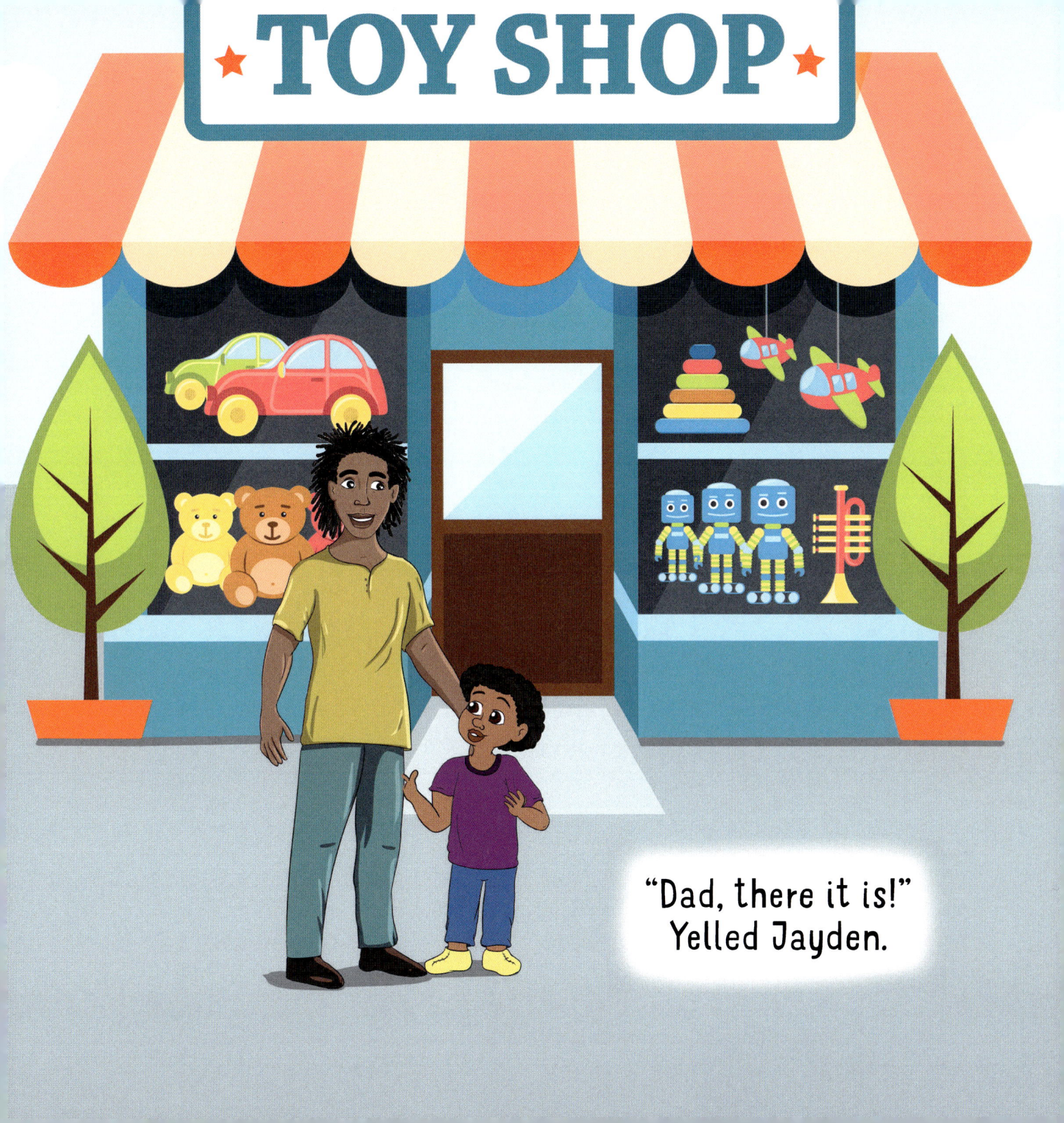

"Dad, I think I want these instead.
"I thought this was the coolest toy ever?" asked Dad.

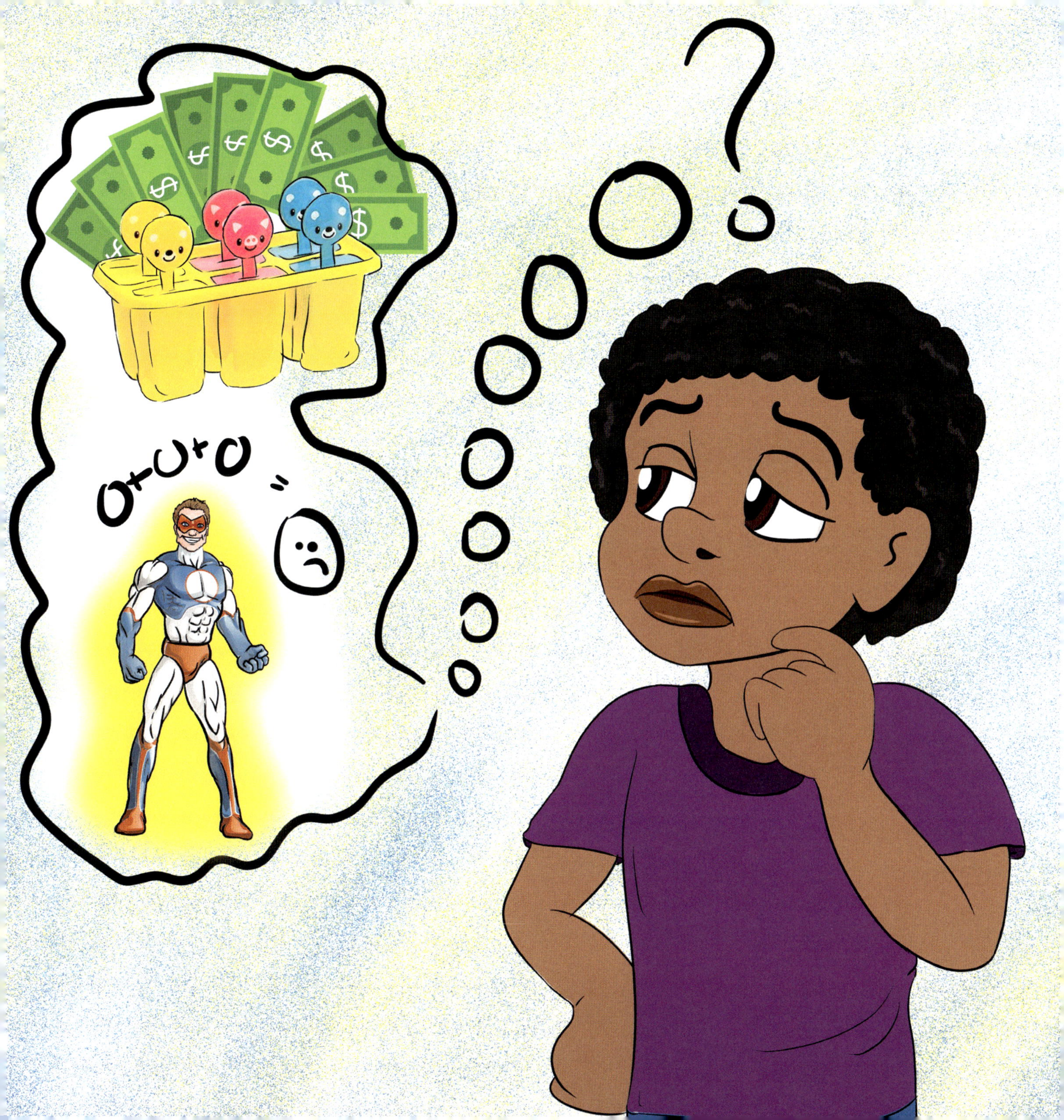
0+0+0 =

"Yea, but I was thinking. My friends like watermelon, but they love popsicles. So I can make even more money."

"I'm sure you can Jayden."

The End

Made in the USA
Monee, IL
21 November 2020

Salmon

Every salmon goes on a long journey. It swims from a stream to the sea and back again. This is an account of one salmon's journey.

Contents

Salmon 4

Eggs – the first stage 6

Alevin – the second stage 8

Fry – the third stage 10

Parr – the fourth stage 12

Smolt – the fifth stage 15

Salmon again – the sixth stage .. 19

The species of salmon 23

Index 24

Oxford University Press, Great Clarendon Street, Oxford, OX2 6DP

Oxford New York
Athens Auckland Bangkok Bogota Buenos Aires
Calcutta Cape Town Chennai Dar es Salaam Delhi
Florence Hong Kong Istanbul Karachi Kuala Lumpur
Madrid Melbourne Mexico City Mumbai Nairobi Paris
São Paulo Singapore Taipei Tokyo Toronto Warsaw

and associated companies in
Berlin Ibadan

Oxford is a trade mark of Oxford University Press

Text © Pierce Feirtear 1999
First published by Oxford University Press 1999
All rights reserved
A CIP record for this book is available from the British Library

ISBN 0 19 915565 8
Available in packs
Animals Pack of Six   (one of each book)   ISBN 0 19 915567 4
Animals Class Pack   (six of each book)   ISBN 0 19 915618 2

Acknowledgements

The Publisher would like to thank the following for permission to reproduce photographs:

Heather Angel/Biofotos: pp 8, 10, 13; Ardea/P Morris: p 14; Bruce Coleman Collection/Charles & Sandra Hood: p 19; FLPA/R Thompson: p 21; NHPA/Agence Nature: p 12; Natural Science Photos/Simon Everett: p 7; Nature Photographers/S C Bisserot: p 15; Planet Earth/Peter David: p 18; Planet Earth/Gilbert van Ryckevorsel: p 20.

Main illustrations, including front cover, by Christopher Tomlin
Background artwork (pp 7, 8, 12, 14, 15, 19, 20, 21) by Peter Bull Art Studio
Titlepage, pp 3, (reused at top of pp 4, 6, 8, 10, 12, 15, 19, 23), 23 by Brett Breckon

Printed in Hong Kong

The Salmon Journey

Pierce Feirtear

What a wonderful fish the salmon is.
No other fish has so many names:
First, alevin... next, fry... then, parr...
then, smolt... then finally, salmon!

Oxford

Two salmon were in a stream. The female salmon dug a nest. The male salmon swam close by.

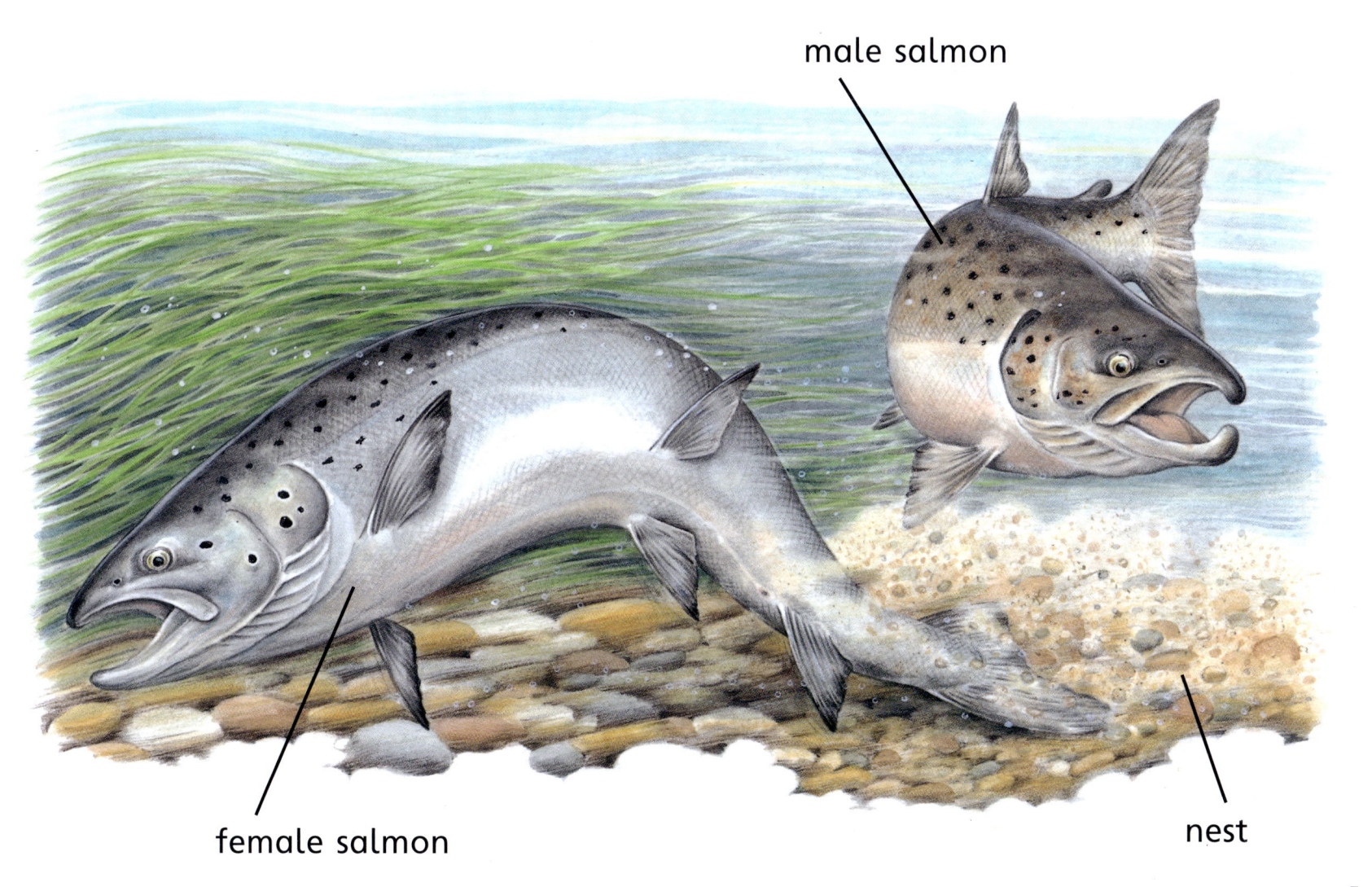

male salmon

female salmon

nest

Eggs

The first stage

The female salmon laid her eggs.

The male salmon spread his **milt** over them.

Then the female covered up the eggs.

The eggs were hidden and safe. After a few months they hatched into tiny fish.

tiny fish hatching

Alevin

Each tiny fish was now called an alevin.

The second stage

An alevin has no **scales**, and you can almost see through it.

One alevin hid in its dark nest. It stayed there for a month. It got food from the **sac** under its body.

food **sac**

Fry

The third stage

At last, the tiny fish swam away. It was brown, and it was now a fry.

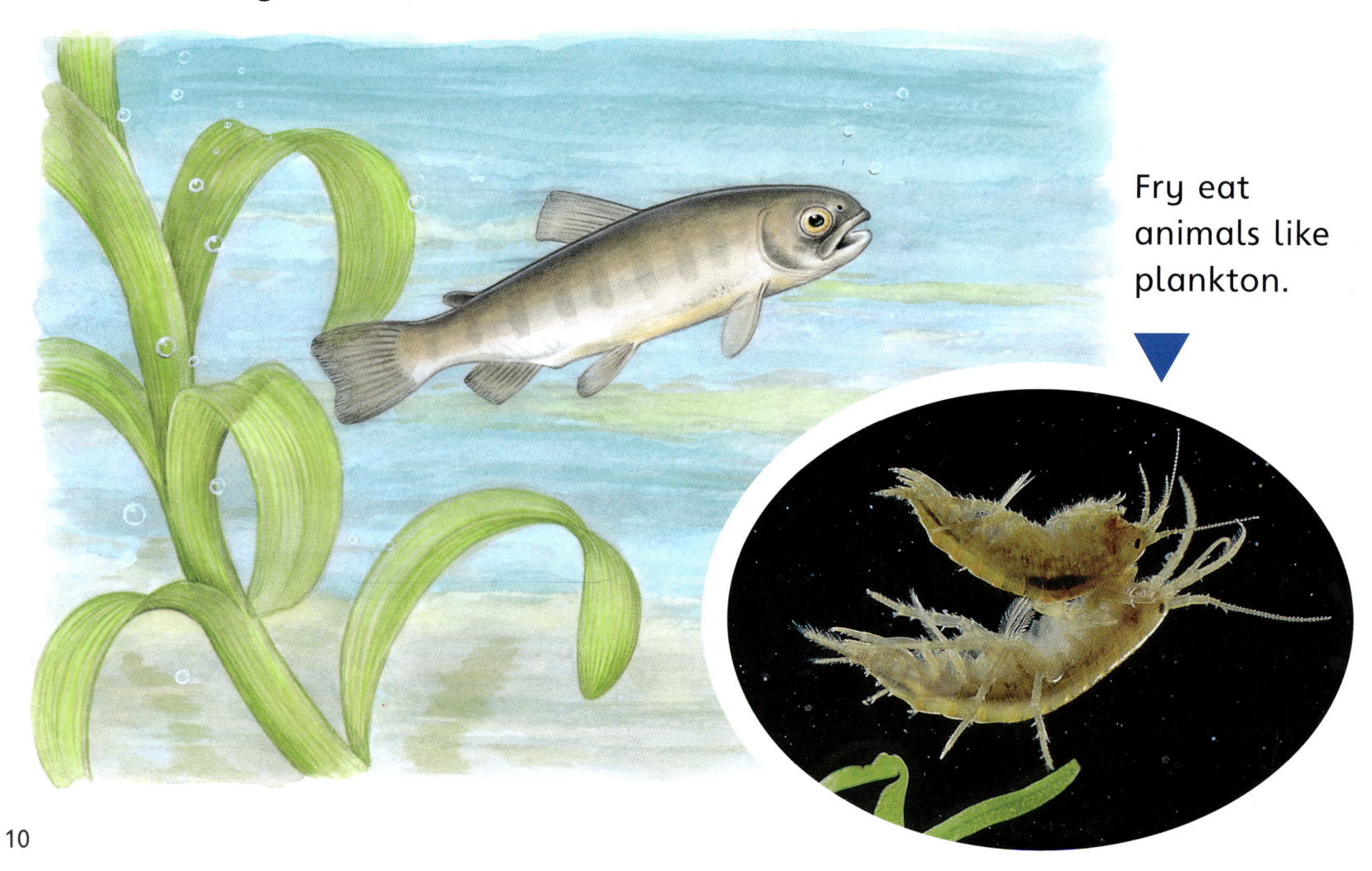

Fry eat animals like plankton.

Big fish wanted to eat the tiny fry. The fry swam close to the sand and stones. Its brown skin helped it to hide from big fish like the trout.

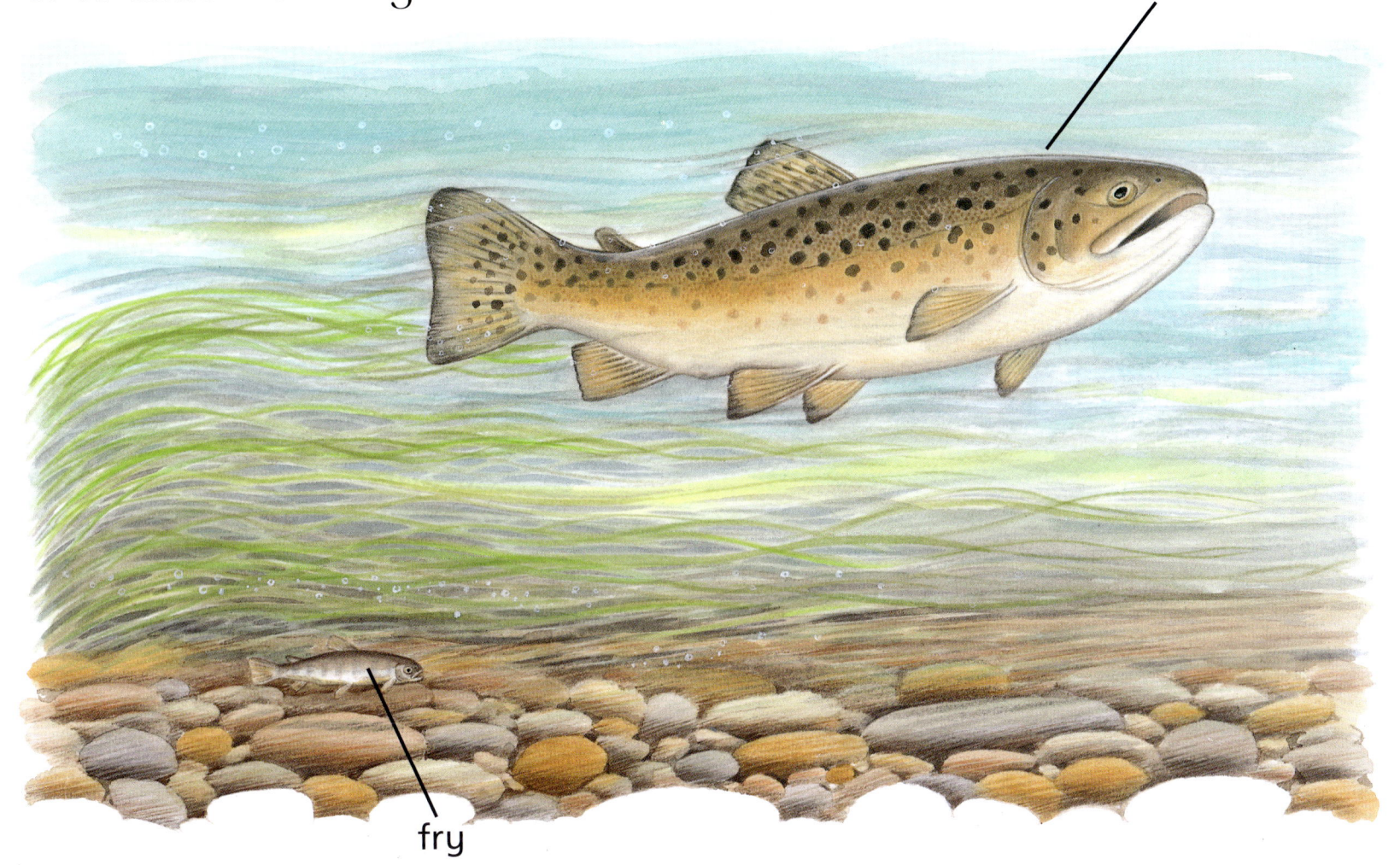

trout

fry

Parr

The fourth stage

The little fish grew bigger and swam down the river. **Scales** grew on its body. The fish was now a parr.

scales

The parr fed and grew. Hungry pike wanted to eat it, so the parr had to swim quickly to get away.

◀ Parr eat animals like crustaceans.

The parr spent a year in the river. It began to change colour from brown to silver.

silver **scales**

Smolt

The fifth stage

The silvery fish was now a smolt, and it was big enough to swim to the sea.

Down, down the river the smolt swam. It reached the mouth of the river. It tasted the salt water of the sea.

In the sea, there were hungry seals and dolphins, hunting for fish to eat. But the smolt's silver **scales** helped it to hide from them.

The smolt was hungry too. It ate the smaller fish, and grew bigger and stronger. Then it swam far, far out to sea.

▲ Smolt eat fish and animals like squid.

Salmon again

The sixth stage

At last, the fish was fully grown. Now it was a salmon, and it was ready to go back to the river.

The salmon swam back up the river with all the other salmon. They changed colour again from silver to brown.

male salmon — female salmon

Swimming up the river was not easy. There were waterfalls in the way. The salmon had to leap high in the air!

At last, the salmon reached the stream. They were ready to make nests. The long journey was over. But soon, it would begin again…

The species of salmon

There are seven **species** of salmon in the world, and they all make long journeys. You have just read about the journey of an Atlantic salmon.

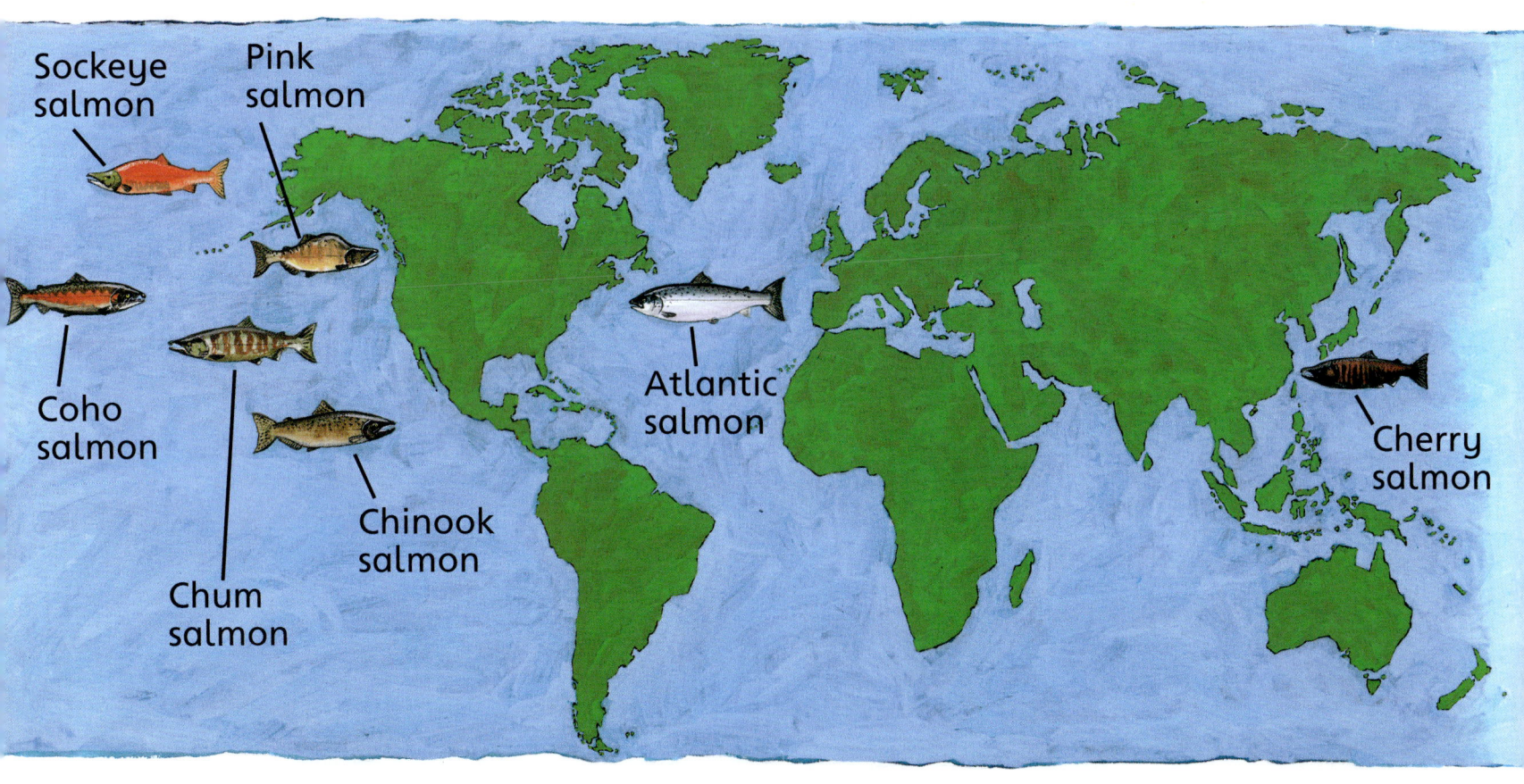

- Sockeye salmon
- Pink salmon
- Coho salmon
- Chum salmon
- Chinook salmon
- Atlantic salmon
- Cherry salmon

a b c d e f g h i j k l m n o p q r s t u v w x y z

Glossary

milt The male salmon spreads milt over the eggs so that they hatch into fish.

sac A sac is a food bag which is in the salmon's egg. The sac comes out when the egg hatches.

scales Scales are thin plates which cover a fish's skin to protect it.

species A species of salmon is a particular sort of salmon. Each species looks slightly different.

Index

eggs 6, 7
female 5, 6
food 9, 10, 13, 18
gravel 6
male 5, 6
milt 6
nest 5, 9, 22
sac 9
scales 8, 12, 14, 17
species 23
trout 11
waterfalls 21